Dickens

Nicola Barber

THE WRITER & HIS TIMES

*C*harles Dickens's birth in 1812 came at a turbulent time in British history. King George III was on the throne, but his mental instability meant that his son, George, Prince of Wales, effectively ruled as Prince Regent. The country was nearing the end of 20 years of war with France – Napoleon was finally defeated at the Battle of Waterloo in 1815. Finally, the Industrial Revolution was changing the way that people in Britain both worked and lived. Not everyone liked these changes. In the year of Dickens's birth there were 'Luddite' riots. Workers broke into factories and smashed the new machinery which, they claimed, would put them out of work.

THE INDUSTRIAL REVOLUTION

Britain was the first country in the world to undergo the changes that became known as the Industrial Revolution. Starting in the late 18th century, small-scale production in workshops began to be replaced by large-scale manufacturing in mills and factories using spinning machines like the one above. New inventions speeded up manufacturing processes, and coal pits were opened up to provide the fuel needed to power the new machinery.

VICTORIAN TOURISTS

The speed with which railways were built across Britain during the middle of the 19th century was amazing. Rail transport was much faster and much cheaper than anything before it; for the first time, many ordinary people could afford to travel. In 1841, Thomas Cook organized his first railway excursion, which went from Leicester to Loughborough. Cook's tours soon became highly popular – this cartoon pokes fun at the people who went on them.

STEPHENSON'S *ROCKET*

The Industrial Revolution also led to a revolution in methods of transport. A major breakthrough came with the development of steam engines that moved on metal tracks. In 1825, a railway was opened between Stockton and Darlington in northern England, proving that rail transport could be both efficient and cheap. George Stephenson, who built this railway, had another success in 1829 with his locomotive, *Rocket*, at the Rainhill locomotive trials. A year later, the world's first passenger railway opened between Liverpool and Manchester.

GREAT EXHIBITION, 1851

In 1851, the Great Exhibition was held in Hyde Park in London. It was the idea of Queen Victoria's husband, Prince Albert, to celebrate the *'Works of Industry of all Nations'*. However, it also showed that Britain led the world in all areas of industry. A huge building, made from glass, was erected especially for the occasion and named the Crystal Palace. Dickens visited the Great Exhibition but did not like it much, saying that *'so many things bewildered me . . .'*

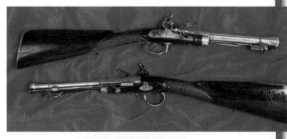

TURBULENT TIMES

In 1839, there was a riot at Newport in Monmouthshire, which ended in death and bloodshed when the military was called in to deal with the protesters. As tempers flared, guns were fired. This was one of the Chartist riots, which marked the years 1838–42. The Chartists took their name from 'The People's Charter', which was drawn up in 1838. Their demands included the right to vote for all men, annual general elections and the right to vote in secret. Chartist petitions were rejected twice by parliament and the movement fizzled out, but some of their reforms were introduced later in the century.

CRIME & PUNISHMENT

Crime and the harsh punishments meted out by Victorian society in response to it, coloured much of Dickens's writings. The family's spell in Marshalsea prison left a mark on Dickens, but even more influential was the prison at Newgate. Newgate was also a place of public execution, where crowds would gather to watch the guilty make their appointment with the hangman's noose. Dickens was repelled yet at the same time fascinated by such brutality. In *Oliver Twist*, Oliver witnesses Fagin in the cells before he is hung at Newgate, while Hugh, Dennis and Barnaby are imprisoned in the institution in *Barnaby Rudge*. The idea of falling on the wrong side of the law, or having a criminal in the family is absolutely central to books such as *David Copperfield* and *Barnaby Rudge*.

HOMES ABROAD

The expansion of the transport network meant that Dickens was able to travel abroad, which he did frequently. He stayed in Lausanne, Switzerland, and climbed Mount Vesuvius (above), where the dramatic scenery left a lasting impression on him. He also visited Paris, and the contrast between the French capital and London installed in him 'a ghostly idea' that was to find expression in *A Tale of Two Cities*.

CLASS & SOCIETY

As Dickens's fame and wealth increased, he and his family moved to increasingly fashionable addresses in London. But although he was a member of polite London society, Dickens was no stranger to the other side of London – the areas of poverty and misery that he knew only too well from his childhood. Even as a prosperous author, Dickens remained both fascinated and appalled by the poor areas of London, and he would often walk the streets of the city at night, observing and thinking. In his novels, he tried to address some of the injustices that he saw around him by bringing them to the attention of the wider reading public in an imaginative form. Many of those injustices were brought about as a result of the oppressive nature of the institutions of Victorian England, such as the law, petty government bureaucracy and the workhouse.

THE WORLD OF CHARLES DICKENS

harles Dickens was born in Portsmouth, but spent much of his childhood in Kent, before his family moved to London in 1822. Dickens came to know London intimately, and the city provides the backdrop for many of his novels. Dickens also travelled widely in Europe, and made two visits to North America, and one of his novels, *Martin Chuzzlewit*, is set in America. Wherever he went, Dickens was a keen observer of all human life, from the poorest to the wealthiest in 19th-century society. It was this keen eye, as well as a vivid imagination and a sense of the comic that inspired much of his writing.

THE WORLD OF THE THEATRE

From an early age, Dickens was intrigued by the theatre. He saw productions at the Covent Garden Theatre and Drury Lane in London, and also at the local Theatre Royal in Rochester (above). He also visited 'private theatres', where anyone could walk the boards for a small fee. Dickens delighted in not only the plays themselves, but also the often poor quality of the acting. This influenced his writing, where his comedy centred around the difference between life's ideals and the rather different realities.

EARLY READING

Dickens was heavily influenced by writers such as Henry Fielding, but equally by folk tales and legends such as Little Red Riding Hood. Dickens wrote that *'Little Red Riding Hood was my first love. I felt that if I could have married her, I should have known perfect bliss.'* The directness of the storytelling, the 'larger than life' characters and the powerful flights of imagination characterize much of his writing.

DICKENS'S CONTEMPORARIES

*D*ickens had a wide circle of friends, including many of the most prominent writers, artists, actors and politicians of the day. Dickens also met some notable literary figures on his travels, including Edgar Allan Poe and Henry Wadsworth Longfellow. One of Dickens's greatest admirers, the Danish writer Hans Christian Andersen, was thrilled to be invited to visit Gad's Hill. Unfortunately, Andersen outstayed his welcome, prompting Dickens to write on a card: *'Hans Christian Andersen slept in this room for five weeks, which seemed to the family ages!'*

WILLIAM THACKERAY (1811–63)

William Thackeray is best known for his novel *Vanity Fair*, published in 1847. Dickens and Thackeray were friendly and praised each other's work, but there seems to have been some rivalry or unease between the two authors. This came to a head in a quarrel in 1858, the same year that Dickens left his wife, Catherine, to whom Thackeray was sympathetic.

The estrangement between the two men lasted until shortly before Thackeray's death in 1863. At Thackeray's funeral, Dickens was described as having *'a look of bereavement on his face which was indescribable'*.

WILKIE COLLINS (1824–89)

Wilkie Collins is best remembered today as the author of *The Moonstone* and *The Woman in White*. This illustration shows him pasting up a poster for the latter. He contributed to Dickens's weekly periodicals, *Household Words* and *All The Year Round*, and worked with Dickens on a number of short stories. Collins's brother, Charles, married Dickens's daughter, Kate, in 1860. However, Dickens disapproved of the match because Charles Collins suffered from poor health.

ALFRED LORD TENNYSON (1809-92)

This image appeared on the cover of Tennyson's *Idylls of the King*, a series of verses on the legends of King Arthur, in 1875. Dickens knew and admired Tennyson's poetry. We know that he read *Idylls of the King* during the same summer that he was busy writing *A Tale of Two Cities*, in 1859. Tennyson visited the Dickens family when they were living in Switzerland, not long after Dickens had christened his sixth child Alfred d'Orsay Tennyson Dickens in honour of the poet.

ANTHONY TROLLOPE (1815-82)

Anthony Trollope's father was a failed lawyer who died young, forcing his mother, Frances, to turn to writing in order to provide for her family. Trollope followed in her footsteps, having his first real success with *The Warden*, published in 1855. This was the first in a series, known as the Barchester Novels. In *The Warden*, Trollope based the character of the editor of *The Jupiter* on Dickens. Trollope later referred to Dickens as 'Mr Popular Sentiment'.

GEORGE ELIOT (1819–80)

George Eliot was the pen-name used by Mary Ann Evans, one of the greatest of the Victorian novelists and much admired by Dickens. She and Dickens met several times. After he read her novel, *Adam Bede*, he wrote: '*The conception of Hetty's character is so extraordinarily subtle and true, that I laid the book down fifty times, to shut my eyes and think about it.*' Dickens tried to persuade Eliot to write a story for publication in *All The Year Round*, but was unsuccessful.

JOHN & ELIZABETH DICKENS

When Dickens was born, his father John was working in the Naval Pay Office at the dockyard in Portsmouth. His mother, Elizabeth, was just 23. They had married in 1809 in the church of St. Mary-le-Strand, and this entry from the marriage register records the event. Elizabeth had another six children over the next 15 years, two of whom died in infancy. John Dickens was an easy-going and hospitable man, who was incapable of living within his means and was always in debt. More than once the family was forced to move house – either because he could not pay the rent or to escape angry creditors.

DICKENS'S BIRTHPLACE

Dickens was born in this house on the outskirts of Portsmouth. The family did not stay here for very long after his birth. Five months later they were on the move, the first of many upheavals that marked Dickens's childhood. The house still stands today, and is open to the public.

TIMELINE

1812
Birth of Charles John Huffam Dickens.

1817
Dickens family move to Chatham, Kent.

1822
Dickens family move to London.

1824
Dickens sent to work in Warren's Blacking Factory; father arrested for debt and imprisoned.

1827
Dickens starts work as a solicitor's clerk.

LIFE IN CHATHAM

In 1817, when Dickens was five, the family moved to Chatham in Kent, a bustling naval town near to the cathedral town of Rochester. This was the most settled period of Dickens's childhood. In 1822, however, this happy period came to an end when John Dickens was transferred to a new job in London, and the family moved to a small, shabby house in Bayham Street in Camden Town.

THE WRITER'S LIFE

*T*hroughout Dickens's childhood, the family was constantly dogged by money problems. Consequently, Dickens was sent to work in a shabby factory when he was 12, an experience that was to haunt him for the rest of his life.

SIBLING RIVALRY

In London, the family's financial problems grew steadily worse. The only respite for John and Elizabeth Dickens was the musical success of Dickens's favourite sister, Fanny. At the age of 11, she was accepted as a boarder at the Royal Academy of Music in London (above). When Fanny left to begin her training as a pianist and singer, Dickens was left behind in the backstreets of London to survive as best he could.

THE BLACKING FACTORY

As the family fell further and further into debt, the situation hit Dickens particularly hard. There was no money for him to go to school, but worse was to come. In 1824, John Dickens decided to accept an offer from a family relation for his son to work at Warren's Blacking factory at Hungerford Stairs in London (above). The job of 12-year-old Dickens was to cover the pots of boot blacking with paper and paste labels on to them. It was a time of utter misery for him. He later wrote of his feelings during this period: *'No words can express the secret agony of my soul.'*

FROM CHILD TO MAN

This portrait of the 18-year-old Dickens, painted by his aunt, Janet Barrow, is one of the earliest known. By the age of 18, he had already seen and experienced a great deal. While working in the blacking factory, his father was arrested for debt and the whole family, except for Charles and Fanny, were forced to move to Marshalsea debtor's prison. Dickens lived alone in lodgings in poverty. After a few months, a legacy released the family from prison and Dickens from the factory. In the following years he attended school and then became a solicitor's clerk. But he already had a different career in mind – journalism.

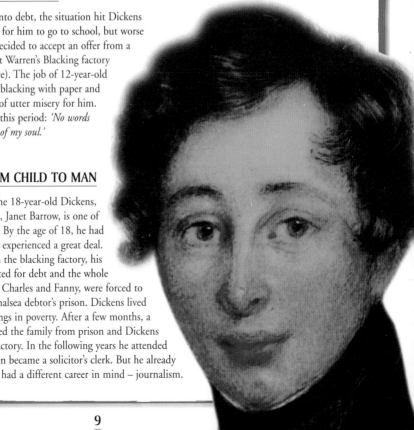

SKETCHES BY BOZ

After his first published article in 1833, Dickens continued to write sketches of London life for the *Monthly Magazine*. In August 1834, Dickens took up a post as a journalist on a newspaper called the *Morning Chronicle*. The editor of the paper encouraged him to carry on writing his sketches, which Dickens did under the name of 'Boz'. In 1836, a collection of these sketches, with illustrations by the well-known artist George Cruikshank, appeared under the name, *Sketches by Boz*. One of Cruikshank's illustrations for the book is shown here.

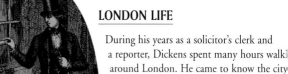

LONDON LIFE

During his years as a solicitor's clerk and a reporter, Dickens spent many hours walking around London. He came to know the city streets and its inhabitants intimately. He began to put this detailed knowledge to good use by writing sketches of London life in all its variety. The first of these sketches to be accepted for publication appeared in the *Monthly Magazine* in 1833. This picture shows the young, hopeful Dickens posting his contribution into the editor's box.

TIMELINE

1830
Dickens meets Maria Beadnell.

1832
Dickens becomes a parliamentary shorthand reporter.

1833
Relationship with Maria Beadnell ends; first publication in Monthly Magazine.

1834
Dickens becomes a reporter for Morning Chronicle*; meets Catherine Hogarth.*

1836
Sketches published in Evening Chronicle.

1836
Sketches by Boz; Dickens and Catherine are married.

1837
The Pickwick Papers; son, Charles, born; Catherine's sister, Mary, dies suddenly.

1838
Oliver Twist; daughter, Mary (Mamie) is born.

1839
Daughter, Kate, born; Nicholas Nickleby.

FIRST LOVE

When he was 18, Dickens met Maria Beadnell (left), the daughter of a banker. He quickly fell deeply in love with her. However, her parents seem to have disapproved of the match – after all, no matter how ambitious Dickens was, he was still the son of a debtor. Dickens was eventually rejected by Maria. The episode affected him deeply, and he was later to draw on it to write the fictional account of David's love for Dora in his novel *David Copperfield*.

MARRIAGE & EARLY SUCCESS

*T*he 1830s were a significant time in Dickens's life. He fell in love for the first time, married and started a family, and his compositions began to be accepted for publication. His first published book was *Sketches by Boz*, which came out in 1836. At the same time, Dickens was already working on the monthly instalments of the book that really made his name, *The Pickwick Papers*. By the end of the decade he was a well-established and highly successful author.

THE HOGARTHS

The illustration above by Maclise shows Dickens with Catherine and Georgina Hogarth. Dickens met the Hogarth family in late 1834, after the journalist and music critic, George Hogarth, moved to London to work on the *Morning Chronicle*. Hogarth soon became editor of the *Evening Chronicle*, employing Dickens on his paper. Hogarth had a large family, and Dickens started to pay particular attention to his eldest daughter, Catherine (above middle). The two were soon engaged, although they did not marry for another year, in April 1836.

DICKENS'S PARLIAMENTARY CAREER

In 1827, Dickens left school and went to work as a solicitor's clerk. The work was deadly dull, and Dickens was determined to move on. He taught himself to write shorthand, mastering the dots, lines and squiggles in only a few months. By 1832, he had secured a position as a shorthand reporter in the original Houses of Parliament, which burned down soon after he left, and were replaced by the buildings on the left. His job was to note down parliamentary debates, and he soon had a reputation as one of the fastest and most accurate reporters ever seen in parliament.

A MOURNED FRIEND

This painting shows Catherine Hogarth's sister, Mary, who died at just 17 years of age in 1837. Dickens was very fond of Mary, describing her as 'a dear friend', and her death affected him deeply. Dickens experienced recurring dreams and visions of Mary 'sometimes as still living; sometimes as returning from the world of shadows to comfort me; always as being beautiful, placid and happy'. The words Dickens wrote for her epitaph, where he described her as 'young, beautiful and good', occur several times in his books. Florence Dombey is described this way in Dombey and Son, *while in* The Old Curiosity Shop, *Little Nell's death draws the same reaction.*

TRAVELS & FAME

ickens's endless energy meant that he was always working on several different projects, whether it be writing novels and plays or editing magazines. Sometimes his hectic schedule landed him in trouble when he could not fulfil his many obligations. Part of the pressure came from the fact that all of his novels were first published in instalments (mostly monthly, sometimes weekly), before being issued in book form. This method of publication brought his work to a wide audience. Soon every instalment of a new story by Dickens was keenly anticipated by an adoring public.

THE HEIRESS

In 1837, Angela Burdett-Coutts inherited a huge fortune from her grandfather, the banker Thomas Coutts. At about this time she met Charles Dickens, and she would consult him on how best to spend money on improving the lot of the poor (see page 27). She became a close family friend, even paying for Dickens's eldest son, Charley, to be educated at Eton. But when Dickens separated from Catherine, relations cooled between the two friends.

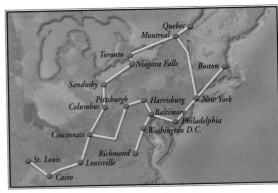

AMERICAN TRAVELS

Dickens's fame spread quickly beyond Britain and in January 1842, he and Catherine set off for a six-month tour of North America. Wherever they went, the streets were lined with onlookers wanting to catch a glimpse of the celebrity author, and invitations to dinners, receptions and balls poured in. Dickens and Catherine travelled to the West by train and paddleboat, and also visited the Niagara Falls in the north.

FAMILY LIFE

This portrait, painted in 1842 by Daniel Maclise shows the four eldest Dickens children: Charley, Mamie, Kate and Walter. Between 1837 and 1852, Catherine Dickens gave birth to ten children; three girls and seven boys. The youngest girl, Dora, was born in 1850 but died suddenly the following year. Dickens was distraught, particularly as his father had also recently died.

TIMELINE

1840
The Old Curiosity Shop.

1841
Barnaby Rudge*; son, Walter, is born.*

1842
Dickens and Catherine tour North America; American Notes *(journal of his American travels).*

1843
A Christmas Carol.

1844
Martin Chuzzlewit*; son, Francis, born; Dickens family live in Italy;* The Chimes.

1845
Son, Alfred, is born.

1846
Dickens family in Switzerland and France.

1847
Son, Sydney, born; family move back to London.

1848
Dombey and Son.

1849
Son, Henry, is born.

1850
Household Words *begins publication; daughter, Dora, born;* David Copperfield.

1851
Dora dies.

1852
Bleak House*; son, Edward, is born.*

1853
Dickens gives first public readings.

1854
Hard Times.

DICKENS AT WORK

Dickens's capacity for work was quite amazing. His publishers were constantly pressing him for a new novel, and he had many commitments as a journalist and editor. In addition, Dickens's frequent involvement in writing plays and theatrical productions placed further demands on his time. Many of the millions of words that poured from his imagination were written at this desk.

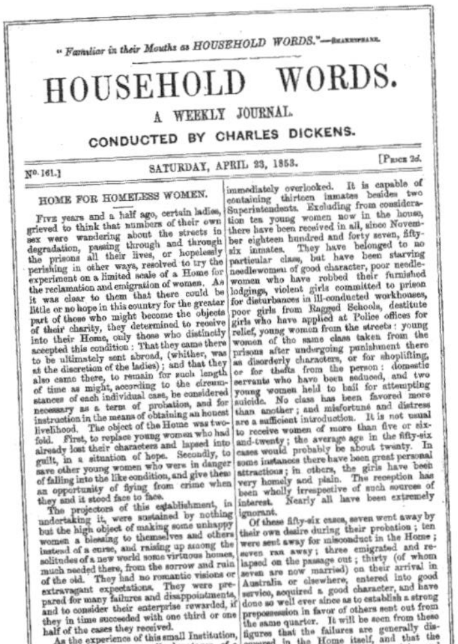

"Familiar in their Mouths as HOUSEHOLD WORDS."—Shakespeare.

HOUSEHOLD WORDS.

A WEEKLY JOURNAL.

CONDUCTED BY CHARLES DICKENS.

No. 161.] SATURDAY, APRIL 23, 1853. [Price 2d.

HOME FOR HOMELESS WOMEN.

Five years and a half ago, certain ladies, grieved to think that numbers of their own sex were wandering about the streets in degradation, passing through and through the prisons all their lives, or hopelessly perishing in other ways, resolved to try the experiment on a limited scale of a Home for the reclamation and emigration of women. As it was clear to them that there could be little or no hope in this country for the greater part of those who might become the objects of their charity, they determined to receive into their Home, only those who distinctly accepted this condition: That they came there to be ultimately sent abroad, (whither, was at the discretion of the ladies); and that they also came there, to remain for such length of time as might, according to the circumstances of each individual case, be considered necessary as a term of probation, and for instruction in the means of obtaining an honest livelihood. The object of the Home was two-fold. First, to replace young women who had already lost their characters and lapsed into guilt, in a situation of hope. Secondly, to save other young women who were in danger of falling into the like condition, and give them an opportunity of flying from crime when they and it stood face to face.

The projectors of this establishment, in undertaking it, were sustained by nothing but the high object of making some unhappy women a blessing to themselves and others instead of a curse, and raising up among the solitudes of a new world some virtuous homes, much needed there, from the sorrow and ruin of the old. They had no romantic visions or extravagant expectations. They were prepared for many failures and disappointments, and to consider their enterprise rewarded, if they in time succeeded with one third or one half of the cases they received.

As the experience of this small Institution, even under the many disadvantages of a beginning, may be useful and interesting, this paper will contain an exact account of its progress and results.

It was (and is) established in a detached house with a garden. The house was never designed for any such purpose, and is only adapted to it, in being retired and not immediately overlooked. It is capable of containing thirteen inmates besides two Superintendents. Excluding from consideration ten young women now in the house, there have been received in all, since November eighteen hundred and forty seven, fifty-six inmates. They have belonged to no particular class, but have been starving needlewomen of good character, poor needlewomen who have robbed their furnished lodgings, violent girls committed to prison for disturbances in ill-conducted workhouses, poor girls from Ragged Schools, destitute girls who have applied at Police offices for relief, young women from the streets: young women of the same class taken from the prisons after undergoing punishment there as disorderly characters, or for shoplifting, or for thefts from the person: domestic servants who have been seduced, and two young women held to bail for attempting suicide. No class has been favored more than another; and misfortune and distress are a sufficient introduction. It is not usual to receive women of more than five or six-and-twenty; the average age in the fifty-six cases would probably be about twenty. In some instances there have been great personal attractions; in others, the girls have been very homely and plain. The reception has been wholly irrespective of such sources of interest. Nearly all have been extremely ignorant.

Of these fifty-six cases, seven went away by their own desire during their probation; ten were sent away for misconduct in the Home; seven ran away; three emigrated and relapsed on the passage out; thirty (of whom seven are now married) on their arrival in Australia or elsewhere, entered into good service, acquired a good character, and have done so well ever since as to establish a strong prepossession in favor of others sent out from the same quarter. It will be seen from these figures that the failures are generally discovered in the Home itself, and that the amount of misconduct after the training and emigration, is remarkably small. And it is to be taken into consideration that many cases are admitted into the Home, of which there is, in the outset, very little hope, but which it is not deemed right to exclude from the experiment.

HOUSEHOLD WORDS

Despite his huge success as a novelist, Dickens cherished ambitions to run a newspaper or periodical – partly as a tool for reform, partly to raise extra income. After some unsuccessful ventures, he launched a weekly periodical called *Household Words* in 1850, which contained articles on a wide variety of subjects. It was a great success and sold up to 40,000 copies every week. Dickens's role on the front page was described as 'Conductor', but in fact he wrote large numbers of articles himself and carefully edited other contributions.

ACCIDENT AT STAPLEHURST

The strange double life led by both Dickens and Ellen Ternan meant that they often met abroad, away from prying eyes in England. Travelling back with Ellen's mother from a visit to France in 1865, the three were involved in a horrific train crash at Staplehurst in Kent. Many people were killed, but Dickens and the Ternans were able to crawl out of their carriage relatively unscathed. A fear of travelling by train haunted Dickens for the rest of his life.

LAST YEARS

In the last decade of his life, Dickens wrote *Great Expectations* and *Our Mutual Friend*. He also left an unfinished novel, *The Mystery of Edwin Drood*, when he died. Dickens died on 9 June, 1870 at Gad's Hill. He had asked to be buried in Rochester, but it was felt more appropriate that he should be buried in Westminster Abbey (see page 28).

LATER LIFE

n 1857, Dickens met a young actress called Ellen Ternan, who was to become his companion for the remainder of his life. A year later, Dickens separated from Catherine. All the children except for the eldest, Charley, continued to live with their father. Catherine's sister, Georgina, who had been part of the Dickens household since 1842, also chose to stay with her brother-in-law, and was his housekeeper until his death. Despite ill-health, the final years of Dickens's life included another highly successful visit to America and public readings from his own works.

THE AUTHOR & THE ACTRESS

When Ellen Ternan met Dickens she was 18 years old – and he was 45. He quickly became infatuated with her, and the strength of his feelings became obvious when he ended his marriage to Catherine. He lost many friends as a result of this affair. Ellen met Dickens's children and frequently visited Gad's Hill, but both she and Dickens kept their relationship as secret as possible to avoid any scandal.

A DREAM HOME

As a boy growing up in Chatham, one of Dickens's favourite walks was past a large house called Gad's Hill Place. Dickens later remembered his father telling him that if he worked hard enough, this house could one day be his. In 1856, Dickens fulfilled his boyhood dream by buying Gad's Hill. He moved into it the following year, and it was his home until his death.

DRAMATIC READINGS

Dickens gave the first public reading of his work in 1853. This was the start of the reading tours that were to become a feature of the last part of Dickens's life, and people would flock to halls to witness the famous author reading excerpts from his short stories and novels. One of the most celebrated of these excerpts was Dickens's adaptation of the murder of Nancy from *Oliver Twist*. Fearing for the strain on his fragile health, family and friends urged him not to perform it. But Dickens was determined, and reported after one rendition that the audience were *'unmistakably pale, and had horror-stricken faces'*.

BOB CRATCHIT & TINY TIM

Bob Cratchit and Tiny Tim are two famous characters from Dickens's first, and best-known, 'Christmas book', *A Christmas Carol*. In this novel, the simple enjoyment of the poor Cratchit family is contrasted with the tight-fisted attitude of the miser, Ebenezer Scrooge. Dressed in threadbare clothes, with his crippled son to look after, the fate of Bob Cratchitt and his family is instrumental in Scrooge's eventual discovery of the true meaning of Christmas.

TONY WELLER

The appearance of Tony Weller in *The Pickwick Papers* ensured the success of the book. Samuel Pickwick meets Tony Weller at the White Hart Inn, Borough. He is described as wearing *'a coarse-striped waistcoat, with black calico sleeves and blue glass buttons; drab breeches and leggings. A bright red handkerchief was wound in a very loose and unstudied style round his neck.'*

LITTLE NELL

Nell Trent is the central figure in *The Old Curiosity Shop*. Her character is drawn partly from Dickens's sister-in-law, Mary (see page 11*)*, who died suddenly in the author's arms not long after his marriage to Catherine. Dickens poured all his feelings into the fictional death of Little Nell, writing to the illustrator of the book *'I am breaking my heart over this story.'*

DICKENS'S CHARACTERS

Dickens portrays all of Victorian society in his novels, from the aristocracy to the poorest of the working classes, and he was a keen observer of humanity. His books are full of larger-than-life characters, but Dickens was also fascinated by ordinary, middle-class people and their often rather shabby, mundane lives. In one of the *Sketches by Boz*, he wrote: *'It is strange with how little notice, good, bad or indifferent, a man may live and die in London. His existence is a matter of interest to no one save himself; he cannot be said to be forgotten when he dies, for no one remembered him when he was alive.'*

GHOSTLY PAINTING

This painting by Robert William Buss is titled *Dickens's Dream*. It shows Dickens surrounded by the ghostly outlines of characters and scenes from his books. After Dickens's death, G.H. Lewes, the partner of George Eliot, wrote: *'the joys and pains of childhood, the petty tyrannies of ignoble natures, the genial pleasantries of happy natures, the life of the poor, the struggles of the street and back parlour, the insolence of office, the sharp social contrasts, east-wind and Christmas jollity, hunger, misery and hot punch – these he could deal with so we laughed and cried'.*

BETSY TROTWOOD

David Copperfield's great-aunt, Betsy Trotwood, is one of the most endearing of all Dickens's characters. She has a sharp tongue and a heart of gold, and wages a daily battle against the donkeys that invade the lawn in front of her house. David notes *'To this hour I don't know whether my aunt had any lawful right of way over that patch of green; but she had settled it in her own mind that she had. The one great outrage of her life, demanding to be constantly avenged, was the passage of a donkey over that immaculate spot.'*

DICKENS AT HOME

Dickens's first proper home as a married man was at 48 Doughty Street (below), just west of Gray's Inn in London. He and Catherine moved there in April 1837. Their household also included Catherine's sister, Mary, and Dickens's brother Frederick. Today, 48 Doughty Street is home to the Dickens Museum. The Dickens family lived there until 1839, when they moved to a rather grander address, 1 Devonshire Terrace, in Regent's Park, (shown right).

CHILD POVERTY

Children suffered particularly badly in the slum districts of London. This beggar child was typical of the street urchins that roamed the streets of Victorian London. Dickens portrays neglected children in many of his novels, but probably the most famous of them all is Jo, the crossing-sweeper in *Bleak House*. This is how Dickens describes him: '*Dirty, ugly, disagreeable to all the senses. Homely filth begrimes him, homely parasites devour him, homely sores are in him, homely rags are on him.*'

DICKENS'S LONDON

Having been in London for two years, I thought I knew something of the town, but after a little talk with Dickens I found that I knew nothing. He knew it all from Bow to Brentford.' These are the words of George Lear, a clerk who worked alongside the young Dickens in the office of the solicitors Ellis and Blackmore. As a child left alone to fend for himself, Dickens quickly got to know the streets and people of London. As an adult, he continued his explorations, often walking many miles at night revisiting old haunts and observing the life around him.

SEVEN DIALS

This engraving of the Seven Dials district of London was made by the French illustrator, Gustav Doré. Doré made many engravings showing the life of the poor in London. Dickens knew the Seven Dials area well. Nearby was St Giles, a slum district known as the 'rookery', where nearly 3,000 people lived in just 95 tumbledown houses without any sanitation. Not surprisingly, conditions in such places were appalling, and diseases such as cholera were an ever-present threat.

NEWGATE PRISON

As a small boy, Dickens often walked past the towering walls of Newgate Prison in London. It haunted his imagination, and appears in several of his works including *Sketches by Boz*, *The Old Curiosity Shop*, *Oliver Twist* and *Great Expectations*. In the historical novel *Barnaby Rudge*, Barnaby is imprisoned in Newgate but is freed when rioters break into the prison and release the prisoners. This novel was based on events in 1780, when the prison was burned down during anti-Catholic riots.

DICKENS & CHILDHOOD

Dickens never spoke about the painful events of his own childhood – particularly his time in the blacking factory – until a chance remark by his friend John Forster caused him to set down an account of his experiences. Dickens did not write an autobiography, but he did use his own childhood as inspiration for *David Copperfield*. Children appear as central characters in many of Dickens's other works, too, including *Great Expectations*, *Oliver Twist* and *Dombey and Son*.

COOLING CHURCHYARD

In the graveyard of Cooling church in Kent lie the lozenge-shaped graves of the children of the Comport family – 13 in all. None had lived beyond 17 months. Dickens often visited this wild and desolate place on the Kent marshes after he moved to Gad's Hill. It provided him with the inspiration for one of his most terrifying scenes, the encounter between Pip and the escaped convict Magwitch in *Great Expectations*.

LITTLE DORRIT

Amy Dorrit, known to everyone as Little Dorrit, is the daughter of the debtor, William Dorrit. In *Little Dorrit*, Dickens drew on his childhood memories of life in Marshalsea, the debtor's prison. Although Dickens and his sister Fanny did not move into the prison with the rest of the family, he was a regular visitor to the prison while his family were there (see page 9). In the novel, Little Dorrit is born and brought up in the prison, and is eventually married in its shadow.

AN INNOCENT VICTIM

A brother and sister form the central child characters of Dickens's seventh novel, *Dombey and Son*. Florence Dombey is unloved by her father because she is a girl. Her younger brother, Paul, the longed-for heir, is a sickly child who dies during the course of the novel. Dickens wrote the death of Paul while living in Paris. '*I am slaughtering a young and innocent victim*' he reported in a letter. The episode of Paul's death was greeted with hysteria by Dickens's public. According to one observer, it '*flung a nation into mourning.*'

OLIVER TWIST

Oliver Twist is possibly Dickens' most famous book. Fleeing the brutality of Sowerberry the undertaker, Oliver goes to London and meets the boy thief, the Artful Dodger, and his gang, shown in this picture. Although Oliver's life is the focus of this novel, Dickens created some of his most memorable characters in the book, including Fagin, Sikes and Nancy.

FACT & FICTION

David Copperfield was Dickens's most popular novel and his personal favourite. It traces the life of David from his birth to his eventual marriage to Agnes. One of the autobiographical elements included in the story by Dickens was an episode in which, after his mother's death, David is forced to work in a warehouse, washing and labelling bottles. It is from this place that David flees to Dover, to throw himself on the mercy of his great-aunt, Betsy Trotwood (see page 17). This illustration shows David having tea at his great aunt's home.

LAISSEZ-FAIRE

In the 19th century, young children were employed to work in coal mines, as the illustration on the right shows. However, it was not until the Mines Act of 1842 that government attempted to put controls on dangerous working conditions. Until then, it was left up to employees and employers to sort out such matters between themselves – a policy known as 'laissez-faire'.

MR GRADGRIND

Through one of the central characters of *Hard Times*, Thomas Gradgrind, Dickens demonstrates what happens when the theory of Utilitarianism is put into practice. Mr Gradgrind believes in 'facts' and facts only – there is no room in his world for imagination or emotion. So, when Mr. Gradgrind asks for the definition of a horse this is what he wants to hear: *'Quadruped. Graminivorous. Forty teeth, namely twenty-four grinders, four eye-teeth, and twelve incisive. Sheds coats in the spring; in marshy countries, sheds hoofs, too. Hoofs hard, but requiring to be shod with iron. Age known by marks in mouth.'*

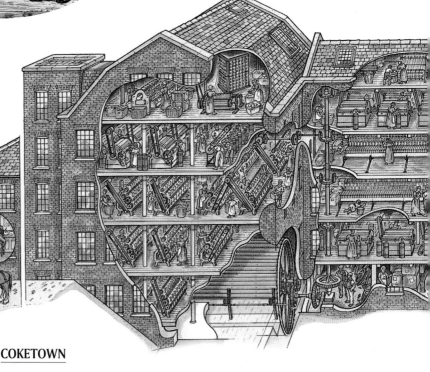

COKETOWN

Dickens sets the action of *Hard Times* in a fictional town called Coketown. It is an ugly place, typical of mill towns and cities that developed during the Industrial Revolution, full of factories similar to the this 19th-century mill in Cheshire (above). Dickens describes Coketown as *'a town of red brick, that would have been red if the smoke and ashes had allowed it. . . It was a town of machinery and tall chimneys, out of which interminable serpents of smoke trailed themselves for ever and ever, and never got uncoiled.'*

DICKENS & THE INDUSTRIAL WORLD

Early in 1854, Dickens attended a meeting with his publishers. Receipts for *Household Words* (see page 13) were down, and the publishers felt a serialized story would help to revive sales. Dickens already had an idea for a new novel – and so *Hard Times* was born. It was published in weekly, not monthly, instalments, a schedule that Dickens found cripplingly difficult to keep to. Consequently, it is one of Dickens's shortest novels.

DICKENS VS. UTILITARIANISM

Dickens set *Hard Times* in the world of mechanized industry. One of his aims was to expose a system of thought called Utilitarianism, developed by the philosopher, Jeremy Bentham (shown above). The slogan of Utilitarianism was, *'It is the greatest happiness of the greatest number that is the measure of right or wrong'*, a theory that paid no regard to the distribution of benefits and burdens. But Dickens objected to Utilitarianism because he thought that it reduced humans to the status of machines, leaving no room for such unmeasurable qualities as imagination or emotion.

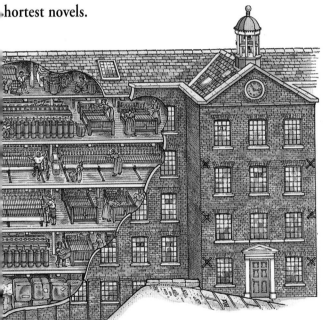

RESEARCHING HARD TIMES

In the cotton mills of northern England, children and women were used as cheap labour. Accidents were common as none of the machines had safety guards to protect the workers. Before starting work on *Hard Times*, Dickens did some research. He had already seen the factories and furnaces around Birmingham; in January 1854, he decided to visit Preston in Lancashire. There, the power-loom weavers from the cotton mills were on strike after a wage claim had been turned down by their employers. In reply, the mill owners had locked out all workers from their factories. Dickens attended a striker's meeting, and Preston provided much of the background detail for the novel. This poster illustrates the plight of such employees.

DICKENS & THE THEATRE

Ever since he was a child, Dickens loved everything to do with the theatre. As a youth in London he considered becoming a professional actor and approached the Covent Garden theatre for an audition. But when the day came Dickens was ill *'with a terrible bad cold and an inflammation of the face'*. However, the theatre and acting continued to play an important part in Dickens's life.

CAPTAIN BOBADIL

Dickens retained his passion for the theatre throughout his adult life. In 1845, he and a group of friends put on a performance of *Every Man in His Humour* by the 17th-century English playwright, Ben Jonson. This painting shows Dickens in the role of Captain Bobadil. The play was performed at a small private theatre in Soho, and the audience included the poet, Alfred Tennyson (see page 7), and aristocrats such as the Duke of Devonshire.

STAGE-STRUCK

During the years that the Dickens family lived in Chatham, the young Charles was taken to see pantomime, featuring Harlequin and Columbine, as well as productions of Shakespeare's *Richard III* and *Macbeth*. He was also taken to see the great clown, Grimaldi (right). His interest in the theatre led him to write a play at the age of 10, 'Misnar, the Sultan of India' based on a story from *Tales of the Genii*, and to spend many hours playing with a small cut-out toy theatre and its characters.

ACTING FOR THE QUEEN

Dickens often put on plays to raise money for fellow writers and artists. He loved everything to do with these performances, not only the acting itself, but also the organization of scenery and costumes, and the conviviality of being in a group of friends. He even took his performances on tours around the provinces. This picture shows a performance of *Not So Bad As We Seem* by Edward Bulwer Lytton, which was given before Queen Victoria in 1851.

THE DICKENS DRAMATIC COMPANY

This photograph shows the Dickens Dramatic Company in 1854. Charles Dickens is the reclining bearded figure at the front. Behind him is his eldest son, Charley, and to the right of him sit Kate Dickens, Georgina Hogarth and Mary Dickens. Wilkie Collins is the stooping figure to the left of Mary Dickens. Collins wrote one of the plays performed by the company, *The Frozen Deep*. It was on a tour of this play, in 1857, that Dickens met Ellen Ternan.

RAGGED SCHOOLS

In the 1820s, a movement started to give poor children a basic education. Run by volunteers (often self-educated themselves), these schools became known as Ragged Schools. Dickens became involved with the Ragged Schools in the 1840s, after visiting one of the schools in Holborn. He was appalled by the dilapidated state of the school, and the filth and stench of the children. Dickens's wealthy friend, Miss Burdett-Coutts duly provided money for better schoolrooms, and she remained involved in the Ragged School movement for the rest of her life.

DEBTOR'S PRISON

A debtor's prison provides the central location for much of the action in Dickens's eleventh novel *Little Dorrit*. Dickens wrote this work at a time when he was increasingly disillusioned with society in Britain. The indifference and selfishness of the wealthy, the corruption and inefficiency of government, and the lack of education and suffering of the poor brought him close to despair. In this frame of mind he created the Circumlocution Office in *Little Dorrit*, a government office whose purpose is *'How not to do it'*, and where nothing ever gets done.

LIFE IN THE WORKHOUSE

One of the earliest issues that Dickens tackled in his fiction was the treatment of children in workhouses like the one below in Alton in Staffordshire. Dickens was appalled by the introduction of the Poor Laws of 1834, and the opening chapters of his novel *Oliver Twist* were intended to draw attention to the suffering caused by these new measures. The new Poor Laws removed payments for able-bodied men and women. At the same time, conditions in the workhouses were made 'less eligible' – more prison-like. Families were split up, and the diet was reduced to cater for only the most basic needs.

A VOICE FOR THE POOR

Dickens knew only too well from his own childhood experiences what it was like to be poor. He was a lifelong campaigner for those who had no voice to speak for themselves, such as child chimney sweeps. He saw the need for better housing conditions, adequate sanitation and access to clean water. All these issues were well publicized in articles that appeared in Household Words *and* All The Year Round.

DICKENS & REFORM

ickens's years as a solicitor's clerk and parliamentary journalist left him deeply sceptical about the possibilities for reform through institutions such as the legal system or government. He preferred to set up projects such as Urania Cottage in Shepherd's Bush, London, a home for homeless women. He did this with the backing of Angela Burdett-Coutts' considerable fortune (*see page 12*), and oversaw the project for several years.

DOTHEBOY'S HALL

In 1838, Dickens made a brief trip to Yorkshire to see for himself one of the many boarding schools that had become notorious for their neglect and cruelty. Many children died as a result of their treatment at the hands of brutal teachers. Dickens went to a school in Bowes run by a man called William Shaw who, not surprisingly, was unwilling to help the novelist in his enquiries. But Dickens saw enough, and the result was the fictional Dotheboy's Hall (as illustrated above), the grim establishment in *Nicholas Nickleby* where Nicholas works as assistant to the sadistic Mr Squeers.

CHARLES DICKENS
BORN 7TH FEBRUARY 1812
DIED 9TH JUNE 1870

THE WRITER'S INFLUENCE

Dickens's writing influenced many of his contemporaries, and has continued to inspire novelists ever since. But his influence was not confined to English writers and speakers. He was truly an international celebrity, and his novels were translated into many languages and read in many countries.

AN ENGLISH GENIUS

The death of Dickens sent people the world over into mourning. The American poet, Longfellow, remarked, *'It is no exaggeration to say that this whole country is stricken with grief.'* Dickens's status as a genius of English literature was immediately acknowledged by demands that he be buried not in Rochester, as he had requested, but in Poet's Corner in Westminster Abbey. An article in *The Times* confirmed the public mood: *'Westminster Abbey is the peculiar resting place of English Literary genius, and among those whose sacred dust lies there, very few are more worthy than Charles Dickens of such a home.'* He was buried in Westminster Abbey on 16th June 1870.

GEORGE GISSING

The novelist George Gissing was 13 when Dickens died. Gissing was greatly influenced by Dickens's writing, and dealt with similar subjects – the poor and the deprived – in many of his own novels. He wrote a study of Dickens's work (*Charles Dickens: A Critical Study*) in which he suggested that Dickens's genius lay in his ability to focus people's attention on serious issues through comedy: *'Only because they (the readers) laughed with him so heartily, did multitudes of people turn to discussing the question his page suggested.'* Gissing also shared Dickens's distrust of public institutions.

SCROOGE

Some of Dickens's characters have become famous personalities in their own right. One of his best-loved tales, *A Christmas Carol*, introduced the world to Scrooge, the miser. Mean-spirited, sneering and spiteful at the beginning of the book, by its end Scrooge is a changed man, made to comprehend the error of his ways by the ghosts of Christmas Past, Present and Future. His penny-pinching stinginess towards others, and in particular his employee Bob Cratchit, are eventually replaced by compassion and an understanding of the true meaning of Christmas. Today, he has become so much part of our literary heritage that the word 'Scrooge' is often used to describe a mean or miserly person.

RUSSIAN AUTHORS

Dickens's novels were read the world over, but there was a particular enthusiasm for his works in Russia. Leo Tolstoy, author of *War and Peace* (as dramatised here), read *David Copperfield* in translation and was so thrilled with Dickens's novel that he learned English in order to read it in the original language. Dickens was an influence on other Russian novelists, too, such as Fyodor Dostoevsky and Ivan Turgenev.

DICKENS'S BIOGRAPHER

Dickens's lifelong friend, John Forster, was a lawyer and writer. He wrote the first biography of Dickens (shown above), *The Life of Charles Dickens*. It was dedicated to his god-daughters Kate and Mary Dickens, and it omitted any possibly scandalous episodes in Dickens's life.

OLIVER!

The musical *Oliver!* was a huge hit when it opened in London in 1960, running for over 2,600 performances. It moved to Broadway, New York, in 1963. It was adapted by Lionel Bart, who also wrote the music. The musical was made into a film in 1968. This scene shows Fagin, played by Ron Moody, surrounded by his gang of boy pickpockets. The part of Oliver himself was played by Mark Lester.

A CHRISTMAS CAROL

Perhaps Dickens's most enduring novel is *A Christmas Carol*, which tells the story of the miser, Ebenezer Scrooge. The story has been brought to the screen on numerous occasions. Scrooge was played by Clive Francis (left) in the 1994 stage production of the book.

"When my thoughts go back, I wonder how much of the histories I invented" – David Copperfield

DICKENS ON FILM & IN THE THEATRE

At the time that Dickens was writing his novels, there was no copyright protection for authors. This meant that anyone could adapt or use texts without permission, without having to pay any fee to the author. Dickens spoke out against this practice many times. But there was little he could do about the many theatrical adaptations of his novels that were made during his lifetime. Often these adaptations dramatized only part of a novel or dispensed with some of the characters. The tradition of adapting Dickens's novels for the stage, and later for the screen, has continued ever since.

NICHOLAS NICKLEBY

This picture is of the BBC production of *Nicholas Nickleby*, starring Nigel Havers. Dickens's third novel includes such characters as Wackford Squeers, the owner of Dothebey's Hall, Smike one of the miserable inhabitants of the school, the Crummles theatre company and the Cheerybles.

TV ADAPTATIONS

Dickens's novels have frequently been turned into adaptations for television, usually shown in several weekly episodes. *Our Mutual Friend* was made by the BBC and aired in 1998. It starred Anna Friel as Bella Wilfer, Steven Mackintosh as John Harmon and Timothy Spall as Mr Venus. One critic said: *'Julian Farino, the director of* Our Mutual Friend, *has taken a huge sprawling novel by the scruff of the neck and turned it into a work of art for television.'*

GREAT EXPECTATIONS

Sometimes the plot of a novel is used simply as the basis for a film. This is what happened with the 1998 production of *Great Expectations*. Although the film retained Dickens's original title, and used his plot as a starting point, the action was updated to modern-day New York City, and the names of the characters were different from those in the book. Ethan Hawke played 'Finn' – Finnegan Bell – in a story of love for an unobtainable woman, Estella, played by Gwyneth Paltrow.

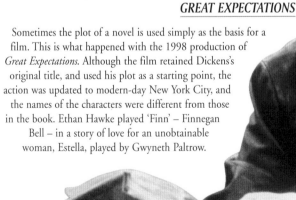

DID YOU KNOW?

Dickens was a very restless person, with seemingly endless energy. He used to walk for miles, often covering distances of 20 or 30 miles at a time.

Twenty years after she rejected him, Dickens's first love, Maria Beadnell, wrote to the famous author. The two former lovers decided to meet, but Dickens was appalled at how much Maria had changed, despite her warning him that she was now '*fat, old, and ugly*'. Dickens recreated the old Maria in the character of Flora in Little Dorrit.

In 1865, Dickens was given an unusual present by a Swiss friend and admirer, the actor Charles Fechter. It was a Swiss chalet – a real, full-size one – in 94 pieces. Dickens had it assembled in the garden of Gad's Hill Place, and he often worked in it during warmer summer months.

Dickens was such a celebrity during his first tour of America that people waited alongside the railway on which he was travelling to catch a glimpse of the famous author. Dickens quickly grew tired of the endless publicity, however. He reported: '*I can't... drink a glass of water, without having a hundred people looking down my throat when I open my mouth to swallow...*'

As a child, Dickens often passed the forbidding walls of Newgate Prison in London, where the bodies of recently hanged criminals were displayed. Later in his life, he attended a public hanging at the same prison.

When he died, Dickens left his last novel, *The Mystery of Edwin Drood*, unfinished. No one knows how he intended to complete this tale, so Edwin's disappearance remains a mystery to this day.

ACKNOWLEDGEMENTS

We would like to thank: Graham Rich and Elizabeth Wiggans for their assistance and David Hobbs for his map of the world.

Copyright © 2003 *ticktock* Entertainment Ltd,

Unit 2, Orchard Business Centre, North Farm Road, Tunbridge Wells, Kent, TN2 3XF, U.K. First published in Great Britain 1998.

All rights reserved. No part of this publication may be reproduced, stored in a retrieval system, or transmitted in any form or by any means electronic, mechanical, photocopying, recording or otherwise, without prior written permission of the copyright owner.

A CIP catalogue record for this book is available from the British Library. ISBN 1 86007 408 1

Picture research by Image Select. Printed in Egypt.

Picture Credits: t=top, b=bottom, c=centre, l=left, r=right, OFC=outside front cover, OBC=outside back cover, IFC=inside front cover

Corbis: 2tl, 3br, 4cl, 7tr, 9cr, 13tl, 19c, 21tr, 24-25c, 26tl, 27br, 30tl, 30bl. Mary Evans Picture Library; 3br, 4bl, 5tl, 6tl, 6c, 14tr, 14b, 16bl, 17tl, 18tl, 18bl, 19br, 20tl, 20bl, 22cr, 23tl, 27tr, 27cr. Alvey & Towers; 2-3c. Image Select International Ltd; 2bl. Art Archive; 3cr, 7cr, 24l. National Portrait Gallery; 6-7b, 12tl. Portsmouth City Council; 8tl. Dickens House Museum; 8bl, 8-9c, 9tl, 10bc, 10-11bc, 11c, 12br, 13tr, 14cl, 16tr, 25br, 29tr. Chris Fairclough Colour Library at Image Select International Ltd; 10tl. Gad's Hill Place; 15cr. Barnardo's Photographic Archive; 18r. Kobal Collection; 20-21c, 28c, 30-31bc. UCL Westminster Abbey; 28tl. Ronald Grant Archive; 29br. BBC; 30cl, 31cr.

Every effort has been made to trace the copyright holders and we apologize in advance for any unintentional omissions. We would be pleased to insert the appropriate acknowledgement in any subsequent edition of this publication.

snapping-turtle
guide